Mexican Clap-Hands Dance

PRIMO

Amazing Grace

SECONDO

Tranquillo ♩ = 96-104

Early American Melody

* Words are printed only when the player has the melody part.

Amazing Grace

Yankee Doodle

SECONDO

Yankee Doodle

PRIMO

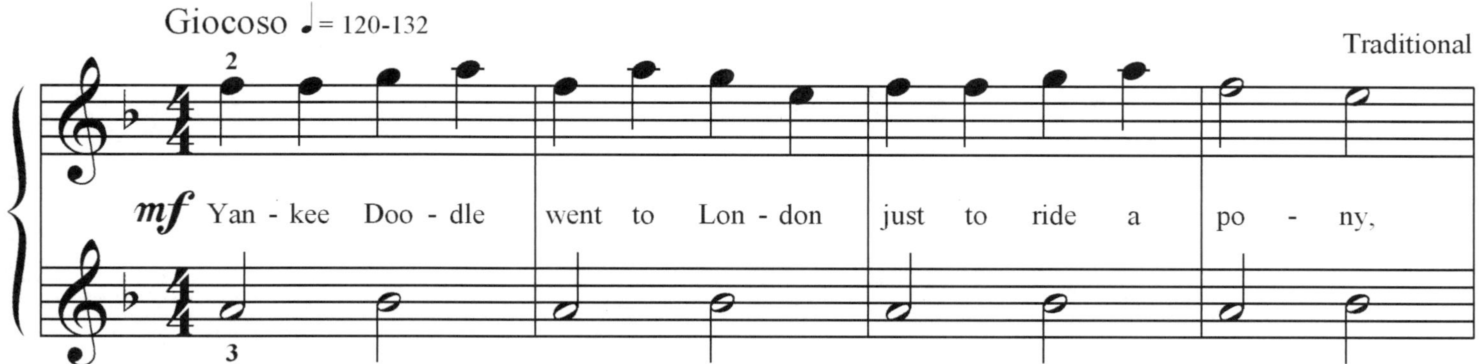

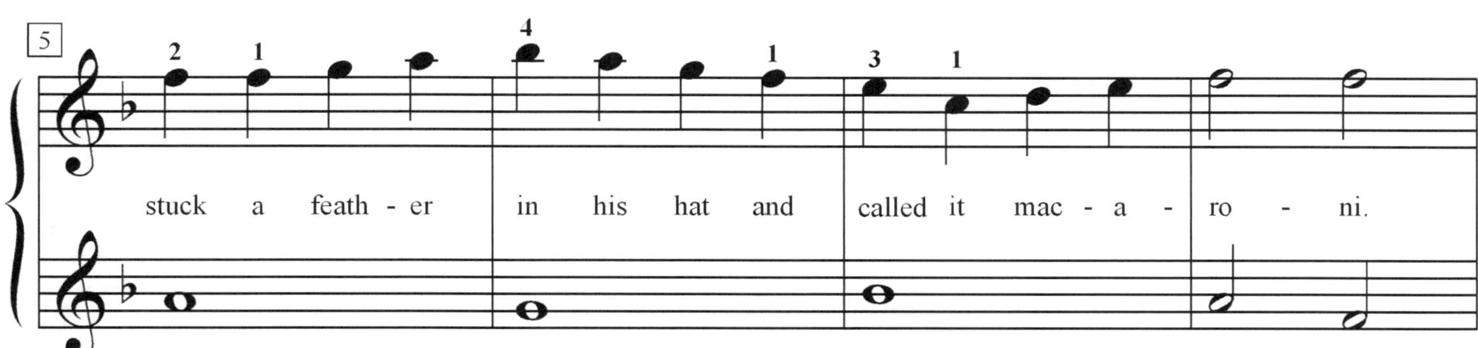

Jazzicle

SECONDO

Andantino ♩ = 104-112

Wesley Schaum

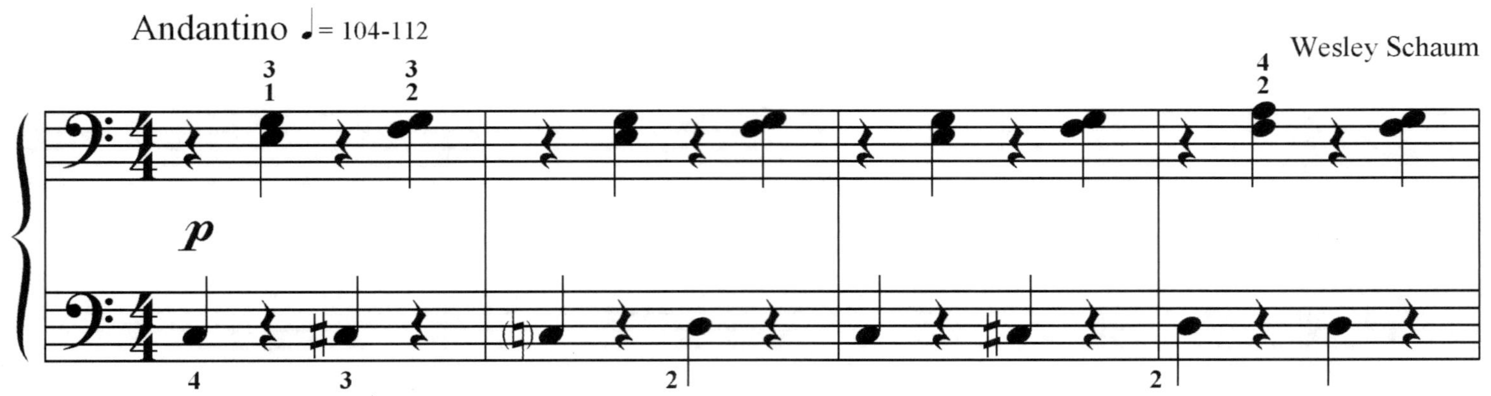

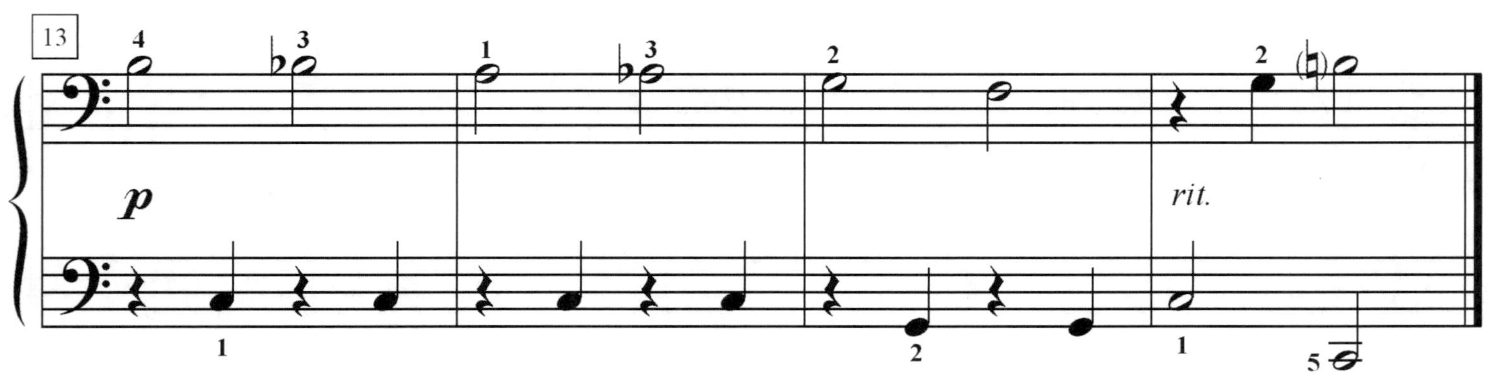

Jazzicle

PRIMO

Andantino ♩ = 104-112

Wesley Schaum

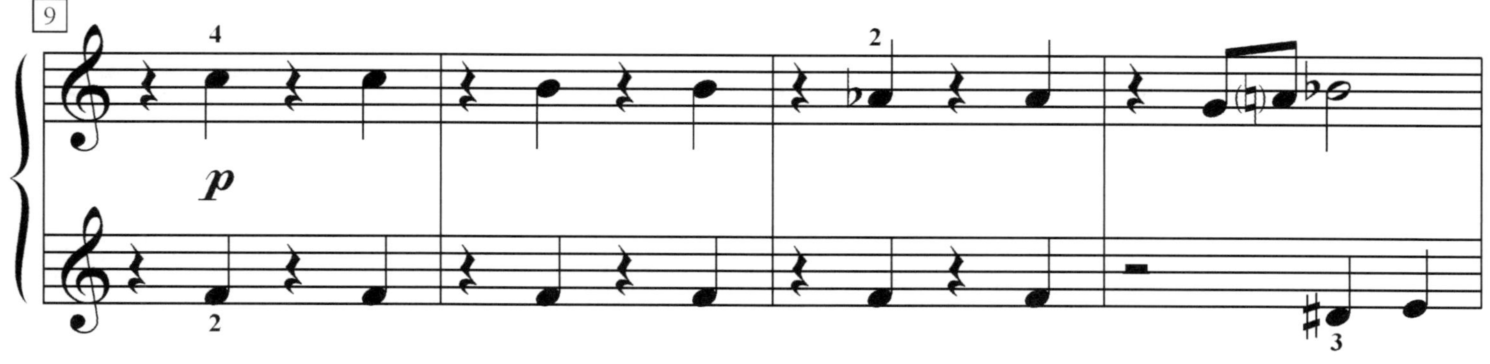

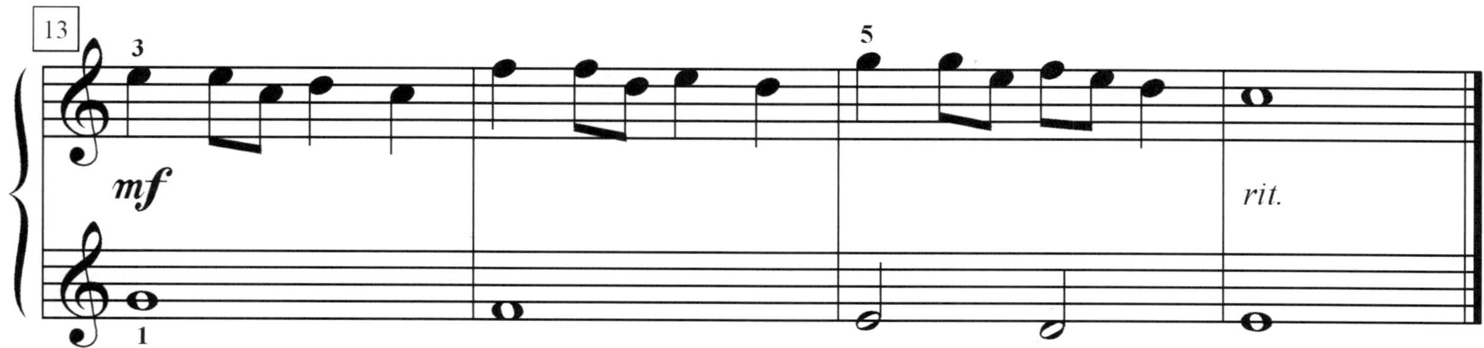

Song of Joy
SECONDO
Maestoso ♩ = 96-104
Ludwig van Beethoven
p
mf
mp